# Float and Scurry

# Float and Scurry

## Heather Birrell

an imprint of Anvil Press

"a feed dog book" for Anvil Press

Anvil Press Publishers Inc.
P.O. Box 3008, Station Terminal
Vancouver, BC V6B 3X5
www.anvilpress.com

Imprint editor: Stuart Ross
Cover design: Rayola.com
Interior design & typesetting: Stuart Ross
Author photo: Kristin Sjaarda
feed dog logo: Catrina Longmuir

---

Library and Archives Canada Cataloguing in Publication

Title: Float and scurry / Heather Birrell.
Names: Birrell, Heather, 1971- author.
Description: Poems.
Identifiers: Canadiana 20190153717 | ISBN 9781772141450 (softcover)
Classification: LCC PS8553.I792 F56 2019 | DDC C811/.54—dc23

---

Printed and bound in Canada

Represented in Canada by Publishers Group Canada
Distributed in Canada by Raincoast Books; in the U.S. by Small Press Distribution (SPD)

The publisher gratefully acknowledges the financial assistance of the Canada Council for the Arts, the Canada Book Fund, and the Province of British Columbia through the B.C. Arts Council and the Book Publishing Tax Credit.

The Canada Council | Le Conseil des Arts
for the Arts | du Canada

BRITISH COLUMBIA
ARTS COUNCIL
An agency of the Province of British Columbia

Canadä

*In memory of two dear members of my Fife family:*

*Margaret Taylor, 1958–2017*
*Rena Barclay, 1935–2017*

# Contents

## I invite my mother into my dream

It is the dream where I cannot find the room where I have to write a Very Important Exam. We are in a never-ending institutional corridor. We wear roller skates and derby gear.

I'm not sure where to go, I say, as I adjust my knee pads.

Don't worry, says my mother. I have an excellent sense of direction.

This is correct. When I come out of a store in a mall I have no idea where I am, but my mother can find her way back to the parking lot in a jiffy.

In the dream, we are skilled roller skaters. We whizz unimpeded down the long hall.

But it doesn't matter which way we turn—we cannot find room 316. Still, my mother looks awesome in her short shorts, tight tee, and rainbow suspenders. We make the air move as we push through the space.

Can I ask you a question, Mum? Why did you take your computer into the Apple store when you forgot your Gmail password?

The woman in there is really nice. Very helpful, she says. Then she does a super spin and raises her eyebrows.

I struggle to keep up with her. She is being show-offy; the wheels on her roller skates trail stars and snazz. She takes my hand but I shake free.

Mum, I say, did you really believe I would let my kid go to a *taser* tag birthday party?

*Laser* and *taser* are very similar words, she says. Then she looks at me like I am the crazy one.

We slow down to check room numbers. The walls are plastered with reminders and reprimands, all printed on letter-size neon paper. Still no room 316.

Mum, I say, do you remember when the power got shut off in Julie's house and you thought it was because there was an electrical short or an administrative mix-up when in fact it was because she forgot to pay the bill?

Yes, she says. I think I do. Wasn't that funny? This is called Shoot the Duck. She crouches down and extends one leg out in front of her, so I have to stoop to talk to her.

You wouldn't think it was funny if it was me. You would think I was being irresponsible.

Oh, don't be silly, my mother says.

Why is it so hard to talk to you, even in my dream? I ask.

Some of her hair has escaped from her helmet at her temples; she smooths it and smiles. Because I am your mother and I will always be your mother, my mother replies.

Before I had children I would have considered this reply hackneyed and irrelevant. Now I understand it to be sad, wise, and true. I pause to adjust my elbow pads.

When I catch up with my mother, she is grapevining down the hallway, her movements graceful and guileless.

There you are, she says, and takes my hand.

I look closely at her.

Don't squint, she says. Maybe you need a new prescription?

## Decanted

Remember when Eleanor picked up a shell on the beach and said it was her cellphone charger? This is how time is decanted: semi-seriously. Who wears a ring and why perched on the rim of sense and the children stick out their lower jaws like actors watching sparrows bathing carefully in sand. It is always good to have someone meet you at the station, whether you are nubile or decrepit. These are the contents of a man's character: potatoes, sorbet, rhyming kindnesses, street names, tumbles, a hearkening for warmth, something cold and chiming, the nose like a trowel seeking out stars, lampposts, apparatuses, pauses, stems, and stews. A black strap around a runner's chest measures heartbeats, a black strap holds up my jeans, a black strap descends—little did I expect, nor did I foresee—on to his open palm marked with life and future offspring. Clumping, slipshod words branching, pinching off toward truth or shopping lists or traffic signs or trundle beds—oh, how I yearned for those as a child!

## Advice

Eat with stinginess or abandon.

In a small wispy voice, say:

We are all insects

That float and scurry.

This is the fact, the fact of death.

You will feel unhinged and light-footed

Because what is different lays claim

To the piles of dusty dream and loam.

## Bawling Is a Thing I Do

*after James Schuyler's "Tears, Oily Tears"*

Don't worry; sous-cheffing brings it on, dirty air, too little shut-eye, too much screen time, caged creatures, border guards, those signs that say the bus will take you all the way home, if only you'd ask, burly men singing "Solidarity Forever" on patchy picket lines, children singing anything, brain chemicals capsizing, people dying without permission, the story someone posted on facebook where the neighbours of a woman who had been unfairly evicted by an unscrupulous landlord formed a human chain around her house and the just-married couple from across the street fed everyone their wedding cake (my eyeballs go veined and shiny and my nose blotches and swells), tear-proof mascara, cats

## 17 Years Married

I'm sad and won't sleep.

It begins with this: pastel-hued hope,
a partner privy to strategy, intention.
Tricky cacophony of birds, scritch-
scratchings of despair, the spotless
starling, the snake, crushed,
then brown paper packages,
beiges, baby blues, babies…

Yes! But also:

Correct rock ledge, three-
tiered whinny, whistlings,
raucous Spanish coins,
indignant greens and oranges—
bristling soft, then querulous, metallic,
a luggage cart, legs, face a dirty round
of chocolate and sleep,
apples plucked from underfoot,
and the red-rumped swallows

who speak to each other
from great distances

## The Time of the Turbot

In Spain, a Canadian passport is a bad toupée.
Still, the tourist feeds and learns from the faltering pail. A guy
could be a geek, a louse, or a yob and still teach us something
of the link between good and evil.

Diving for booze might seem the cachet of aging
mealy-mouths. Not a jot! When terror is breaching. The ocean
warns, roars, is sometimes empty. What a man learns of his home's
circumference is not limited to radius or pi, but might repeat
like raw onions, or keep on after point one four.

When all countries have been axed, we might err
on the side of love and the Atlantic. After all, you can bring a dish
to the zoo, but you cannot make her boil. Anyway, the fish are few
and it's too late to be ad-libbing.

## I invite Mr. T into my dream

I invite Mr. T into my dream. It is the dream where I am flying but my flying is swimming, the air the consistency and density of water. I breaststroke with conviction, my arms and legs moving in repeated circles through the air.

I am swimming over the streetcar tracks, following the streets' iron arteries, floating mere metres above the suspended lines to which the cars are attached, when Mr. T swoops up to join me. Mr. T doing the breaststroke boosts my confidence. Because—let's be honest—I am more graceful than him, my movements more effective. Still, we get into a rhythm, and once we have found it he turns to me.

Thanks for inviting me into your dream, Mr. T says.

This is very Mr. T-ish—to thank *me* when I should be welcoming *him*, as his host.

My pleasure, Mr. T, I say. What do you think? I interrupt my breaststroke to sweep my hand across the sky, indicating the lake, the low-rise brownstones of Roncesvalles Avenue.

It's cool, Mr. T says. Your dream is cool!

I know! Who knew that flying was like swimming? Hard work, really.

You got that right, says Mr. T. In the show, flying wasn't really my thing.

I remember, I say. I ain't gettin' on no airplane, fool!

Uh-huh, says Mr. T. Hannibal had to drug me and drag me onto those things. But I'm okay now.

Mr. T is wearing a large gold medallion, and as we fly it swings down below his squat, muscular body. I wonder if it hurts his neck. We fly together all the way down to Queen Street and across Lakeshore with its line of cars sniffing each other's behinds, until we reach the lake. I've never flown over the lake before, but with Mr. T by my side, I feel brave.

Shall we keep flying? I ask.

Why not? says Mr. T. And when he shrugs, his medallion bobs up and down, glints in the sunlight.

We tilt ourselves slightly upward, strengthen our stroke, then even our bodies out. We fly up and over the boardwalk and its earthbound runners and babies in buggies, the bleached-out driftwood and beaten-down bits of plastic, the cigarette butts and coffee cups, the fierce, gliding swans, the oily-looking cormorants perched on the breakwater.

And then we are out over the wide expanse of Lake Ontario, just me and Mr. T.

Mr. T turns to me. Let's rest, he says, and flips himself upright, legs treading, cycling, giant arms pushing the air back and forth in front of him.

I begin treading too, but using the eggbeater, which I learned as an amateur synchronized swimmer in high school.

Cool technique, Mr. T says, and grunts approvingly.

There is silence while we take in the vastness of the water below us, the depth and width of the horizon.

My dad met you once, you know, I say.

Mr. T does not look surprised. I meet a lot of people, he says.

Yeah, I say. It was in the factory where he worked. They were going to shut it down and demolish it so they figured why not film some movies there before they turfed all the workers.

I don't mean to, but I am getting angry with Mr. T.

My dad was the local union president and they gave him the job of showing you around. Like, a consolation prize, I guess? I am yelling at Mr. T when really it is not his fault. He is just being Mr. T, aka B. A. Baracus, beloved star of *The A-Team*, which I watched from 1983 to 1987.

Ah, man, says Mr. T. The world sucks.

I swallow hard because I don't want to cry in front of Mr. T.

I wake up and remember that when I asked my dad about meeting Mr. T on the factory floor, he said Mr. T was a really nice guy.

## You Are Not Obliged

"So apart from your sister, and apart from Lenin and Jesus,
you have no close friends in the whole world? Never mind.
You are not obliged to answer."
—Amos Oz, *Judas*

Dear March,

The Keele bus flees from my waving form,
mitts dangling from my pockets like pale tongues.

You are not obliged to answer.

So the sun is shining, so what, you scurrilous,
skulking, wannabe Shakespearean villain!

You are not obliged to answer.

I want to hopscotch over you, feed your mocking
squares into the paper shredder. Ha ha! April fool!

You are not obliged to answer.

An old woman with a walker skip-slunks
across the intersection, avoiding potholes.

You are not obliged to answer.

I will meet you with uncharacteristic sangfroid
in conversation, on subway platforms,
in dangerous glass houses, and in every
slow, saddening burden and jaggedy lack.

You are not obliged to answer.

I dreamed we kept a horse with a clipped tail
and swirling sweet eyes. She was our livelihood.

You are not obliged to answer.

Oh, look! Identical silver laptops,
coffee-shop friend! But you
use yours to book a flight to Barcelona.
Therefore: not friend.

You are not obliged to answer.

In other countries, daffodils or flash floods.

You are not obliged to answer.

The awning of the mud-brown bungalow
across the street, the Board of Education
insignia on the side of that white-panel van, Alyssa's
duffel coat, flecked in Charles's hooded left eye.
(Green. But nowhere else.)

You are not obliged to answer.

Cargo clanks, crows caw. Other, smaller
birds tell secrets in the brush. What do they
know?

You are not obliged to answer.

## Dream Analysis

The extra room is full
of scratched-up
old bureaus and one
large talking rodent
who walks
on his hind legs and
knows much more
than he lets on.
The floor is strewn
with grey
throw pillows.

Common as dirt, the dream of the extra room in the house, unexplored until now. You have pockets of unused potential festering in your subconscious. The rodent is you; the bureaus are you. Your work, if you can handle it, is to get that rodent to speak plain, to pry open those bureau drawers. (Who even uses the word *bureau* anymore?) Can you say *compartmentalize*? That's it. Com. Part. Men. Tal. Ize. Does the rodent have a tail? Yes? Well, you know what that means, don't you? If you guessed: sexual. If you said: repression. If the word *phallic* came to mind, you are disgusting, gutter-minded. Why can't a tail be just a tail? Or a means of balance, a way to encourage nimble, ratlike steps? Also: throw pillows. Barf. You have been looking at too many pinterest pictures and should venture out into the real world where real life will bite you like an oversize rodent in your privileged, pinterested ass.

## The Follow-Up Call Came

The suddenly always happens,
the enchanter's *Umm, right there,*
bulging out of the narrative
like a surprise credit card debt.
No, the other one! The halo
projected on the screen; televised
goodness, this pleasure. Weather,
whether, exciting, exiting. Lashings
of love. Discuss.

Charles would live in that shed
if he could, smoking, making whirligigs,
listening to endless podcasts. Daddy,
tell it again—the story of your
subway humiliation! The other day
he said "we" was his new pronoun;
the collective first person plural
signifying solidarity or chores foisted
upon you. Pesky pause.

Envelopes are miraculous and lovely.
When they are gone, we will miss them.
They set up a repair shop in the church
on the corner like something from
the 1930s. I thought of the junkyard
in the basement, bent spoons and
faulty speakers, but I didn't make it
in time.

It's okay to love books, but don't
swing off the bookcase. Really, don't.

## Snow Day Poem

Listen. February is hard with the world
gone all bridal, but married to what?
Easy to say we are free to whoop and
wander inside our own selves but what if
the toad of tiredness settles in your heart?
What if all those birds of optimism go
unnoticed and the coffee cups in the cupboard
come back tilted? Let me offer you

some things: a sob, a slope, a seethe, a hoarse
keyboard. Your mission, if you choose to accept it,
involves civilization, an urn, a cellar, and a cheeky
bit of chocolate. Everybody is so busy building
platforms these days; will they finally
close the schools? It is confusing when men
who look like they belong in locker rooms begin
singing Leonard Cohen songs to children. Confusing

and exquisite. So here's the thing: we have no money
and I still want to buy that puffy, overpriced muffin.
The library remains open. I finally have a lip balm
in every coat and purse pocket. I dreamed
I protected my youngest child from the blades
of a snowplow. We were on a beach and it was not
a snowplow. The loudest thing I have ever heard?
When my brother-in-law took a sledgehammer

to our cast-iron tub. My kids were often spongy and submerged in that tub. Once they laughed for hours when one of them said "New York Shitty" by mistake. We are all going to be okay until we're not. And the fact that humans can make analogies reminds me of that song about the hole in the bucket, dear Liza, dear Liza. It goes on forever and the bucket never gets fixed

but it's so much fun to sing.

## Flashman

*i*

The filmy-eyed old man went searching for him during the Polish Festival. He had a sister but they had to put her down. On every corner, beautiful girls wearing coronets of red flowers drank beer out of plastic cups.

*ii*

I didn't know when I met you that any of this would happen. We were playing Scrabble on an island closer to Africa than Spain. You used the word *cozy* in a way I had never seen or heard before. We went to see a movie. *La Momia Vuelva.*

*iii*

Desert dog, street dog, half fox, half hare.

Listen. Nails clicking out circles of goodbye, goodbye, goodbye.

## Will

Gone shopping—obviously—so
endure.
My will is in the concertina file.
Remember me, daughter, celebrate
your mother, my proud accomplishments,
my strawberry rhubarb crumble.

Don't vote for that jackass
Ginsberg, and don't
let the kids play too many
social media games.

I'm not actually dying;
I just think it's good to be
prepared and the lineups
at No Frills are really long,
my darling, plus parking
is a nightmare!

## Pro-Suicide Eulogy

I know why you came here today, I do, and I appreciate the respect you are paying to the dearly departed but I wonder—I often wonder—if you have stopped for long to think about the ways in which life on other planets might manifest itself here on earth. If you think my words are tangential to your present concerns, I beg you to reconsider, to refresh your feeds, reboot your systems, retract all previous assumptions. Dearly beloved, we are gathered here today because Sheehan put a pistol in his mouth and pulled the trigger. This we know. And we have expounded upon the benefits of compassion, the uselessness of blame-placing, the mysteries of mental illness, and the stigma that billows, bloats, and blasts through our lives. But we have not addressed the wonders of the afterlife. We know in the past that those who sinned in deed by doing God's work by ending their own lives were denied entry to heaven, buried shamefully in spots neither here nor there. But we have reason to believe that those who choose this taboo route in fact find a different more fruitful paradise, a world beyond our ken. Do you want to hear more? Have you no inkling of the phenomenon to which I refer? It is only by volunteering one's life that one can find purpose and insight beyond this veil of sorrows. I am not speaking of oval-eyed, green-tinged men or giant, insect-like predators. I do not truck in Hollywood's tinsel and terror. No, when Sheehan pulled that trigger, he took a step bolder than those who have trodden on our very own moon. He agreed to feel for the other, nether world. And I am forever in his thrall.

## Google Search

Why do some people hate cilantro? *Sadness in childhood.*

Why do some people have dimples? *Sadness in childhood.*

Who wrote "Shape of You"? *Sadness in childhood.*

Why are people racist? *Sadness in childhood.*

Why are fireworks red? *Sadness in childhood.*

Who wrote "Beauty and the Beast"? *Sadness in childhood.*

Why are bees dying? *Sadness in childhood.*

Why do some people react aggressively without provocation while others don't? *Sadness in childhood.*

Who wrote the Quran? *Sadness in childhood.*

Why do some pokemon have a blue background? *Sadness in childhood.*

Why do some people have sadness in childhood?

*They do. They forget.*
*Tastes like soap.*
*Ed Sheeran. Grimm. God, or his messenger.*
*Pure chemistry.*
*We fucked up.*
*Strontium carbonate.*
*Merely an insignificant background image.*
*God's fingerprints.*

# Whale

My father who is not my father,
but someone compact and mustachioed,
takes me out in a boat, in a bay.

There it is! he shouts,
as a whale rears up and out
of the water. And I nod, but
also rear back. So much power
without limbs or machinery!

The whale looks exactly like
my auntie Rena who died of
coughing every time she laughed.
My heart swells
in spots, as if mosquito-bitten.

When the whale dives, it
sucks us down, flotsam
in its barrelling trajectory.

Hang on to the boat, follow
its sucking wake to the surface, my father
(who is not my father) advises. I am not
so easily taken. I plead with him.
He is peppery, convicted.
We are in over our heads.

My stroke is forceful, made of pump and pull.
Persistence: deft deltoids, honed hip flexors.
I elbow my way up the beach
like the first amphibian, then run, loose-
jointed, thumbs brushing thighs,
all the way to Montreal.

## Ode to Our Rusted-Out Red Dodge Dart

Dad must have been lost in a small fact that Friday
you drove us, unhinged and heavy-footed

in a stingy three hours
to the rented cabin

We sat on towels to keep the sweat
from scurrying us off the vinyl

It was July and a thunderclap
knocked three times, changed the script

Think of yourself as a character, you said
when we told you the water was rising

We drew our knees up to our chests
watched the dark slosh below us

There were bundles of childhood
stacked in bales in the fields

If Hollywood can be believed
anything could be out there

## I invite the locked mental health ward at St. Joseph's Hospital into my dream

I do this because I want to look at it in my dream, to hold it like a Rubik's Cube, twist it one way then the other until the colours match. There were boys in Grade 6 who could do this—Oldrick Kuca springs to mind—but I did not have the persistence or futuristic spatial awareness to stick to it for long. What I loved was the feel of the smooth, dense, right-angled plastic, the clicking sound as the squares moved into place. The locked mental health ward at St. Joseph's Hospital is not lovely; it is bereft of accent walls, pops of colour, and soft furnishings. It is gunmetal grey, or sky-before-storm blue. It has a TV in one corner anchored to the wall with an ancient mechanical arm permanently bent at the elbow. I stayed in a cubicle whose dusty privacy curtains were moored to a beige rectangular bar that floated just below the pockmarked panelled ceiling. One day, when I was trying to do yoga, my mat spread like a picnic blanket in the middle of the small space; one of the nurses I liked came by and did a pretend knock, which is when you say *knock-knock* because there is nothing to rap your fingers against. He stuck his head around the curtain and looked surprised when he saw me with my arms stretching up above my head toward the sky, which was apparently still sitting there above St. Joseph's Hospital, where it had always been. Oh, you're doing *that*, he said. That was when I knew I would marry him, except I forgot to get his number even though I was much skinnier and more impulsive then. Plus already married but you know. There were other people in the locked mental health ward at St. Joseph's

Hospital besides the nurses and doctors. These were the crazy or ultra-sad people. One of them had curlers in her hair and kept shouting about a shopping cart and I knew it was mean to think she was an annoying cliché, but I thought it, oh yes I did. Another became my friend. I don't think nurses and doctors like crazy and ultra-sad people to become friends. We are like revolutionaries in the mountains; we get ideas, and sometimes, secretly, and with stealth, we act on them. My friend in the mental health ward at St. Joseph's Hospital was black and gay and his family was evangelical, so it is possible he had better reasons for being there than I did. I wished I could heal him but I was tired and resigned. We did not resent anyone trying to help us, they just seemed so far away. We wished them well! Sometimes I was proud of my illness, in the way the tortured admire the resourcefulness and persistence of their captors. When the doctor upped my sleep meds, I still woke at 3 a.m.—they could not hold me down for long!—and found my way easily to the fluorescent glow of the nurses' station, beggarly palm extended. I can't sleep, I said. And when I close my eyes, I see scary things. Then one of the other nice nurses—the one who told me often and with passion that I was not what I thought I was and reminded me of the only good-hearted person on a small-minded, small-town PTA—gave me two more small blue pills with a paper cone of water and watched closely as I swallowed them. Oh yeah, there was another guy there too! He came a couple of days after I did—white, sinewy, old-school tattooed. He was someone the nurses knew; they looked disappointed in a kind way to see him. His wrists were bandaged and he needed a cigarette. He stared at me with soft eyes but once he put the TV on too loudly and the news was about a military man in the U.S. who had taken over a building and the new guy watched it so matter-of-factly, like he didn't get the clatter it set off inside me. I went into my room with its poor suggestion of walls and lay on my bed. I could hear the announcer announcing and the reporter reporting on the number of dead and I had no means of telling anyone to turn it down, turn it down, turn it off. I was too shy plus it seemed impolite in our shared space even though the shopping-cart lady had had no such qualms. In the locked mental health ward at St. Joseph's Hospital all of the food tasted like a quintessence of dust, but I appreciated the fact that someone brought it to me every day on an orange tray. I think you should know I am better now, which is why I could invite the locked mental health ward at St. Joseph's Hospital into my dream. There are a lot of movies about these places and some of what they show is correct. But also: sometimes people need to be held. Sometimes buildings hold people.

## Carry

When you lose a person,
carry your lost one
in a state-of-the-art baby
carrier whose materials
and technologies have
evolved not only to ease
the pressure on the carrier's back, but
also to maintain the safety
and well-being of the carried—
to ensure their hips
do not splay awkwardly,
that their airway remains
clear, their vision unobscured,

that they may still access
comfort and sleep

## Chair Memory

I am standing next to one of the chairs.
I am about to sit down in the chair.
My hands are on the back of the chair.
My sister is sitting in the other chair.
She is drawing a house with windows
like little jails. It is after supper
and we are in our housecoats. If I stand on
my tiptoes I can see out the window
of the back door. It is nearing night. It is fall.
Outside shadows melt into
other shadows and some of the shadows
are raccoons that lumber big-bummed across
the yard, looking for stuff to eat, digging
up the lawn my dad has laid in squares
of careful green. It is almost bedtime
but not quite and we have already
watched our show and I hate
this feeling of not being in one thing
or the other, all shadowy like the raccoons,
and when I look out the window again
the trees are taking the wind seriously;
they bat at it with their branches,
rustle their leaves madly. Something
rises in me
and walks outside to greet the wind.

## Novel

1.  I don't know why apple slices make me sad, she thought.
2.  This line could begin my novel.
3.  Yes, but you must have an antagonist and a plot graph that looks like a lopsided pointy witch hat. (According to the novel-writing books that make one (who is I) feel grubby and insufficiently goal-oriented.)
4.  Otherwise you will never, ever, ever, ever, ever, ever, ever, ever, ever, ever, ever, ever be successful.
5   When I was hospitalized for my "nervy," as my husband calls it, I had one very bad recurring dream. It did not feel like a dream. I was held prisoner in a dank underground pit. But it was all a big mistake.
6.  Yes! That's good! The descent into the unknown, the dark forest of the subconscious! What are the brambles? How go the quests? In which ways does she fight her way back?
7.  No, she (who is I) says. That place was just fucking terrible. And not even a metaphor. Or maybe a metaphor. I didn't even leave it. Or I did. But it didn't leave me.
8.  Are there other people in your novel? I mean, besides the gloomy, nervy-having, pit-dreaming protagonist?
9.  You know that novels are like dreams, right? So everyone in the novel is the author and the author is everybody.
10. Interesting. How do you plan to work in the apple slices?

11. There is a great story by A. S. Byatt called "The Thing in the Forest," featuring a loathly worm. You should read it because it is better than this and explains things.

12.

13. She stared at the apple slices.

14. Is it too simplistic to say capitalism kills creative writing?

15. I don't know why apple slices make me so sad, she thought.

# I Was Best Prison Librarian

ever seen my way
with books' spines—
line up with dge of
else's understood imptance
of ding, abyss, do, own, concrete
floor, down, absorbed blood
from altercation, alteration, action
between literate criminals' pistent
grim. Also, my voice is very deep,
gives mpression of learnedness,
vernacular, vehicular,
ventricle of current surrounds.
I know my shit.

## I invite my great-great-great-grandfather, the tinker, into my dream

It is the dream where a bad man is chasing me and my legs feel like cement blocks.

My great-great-great-grandfather is a small wiry man with a small wiry moustache.

The bad man is someone I recognize only from headlines and schoolyard whispers. I know that if I stop to talk to him he will convince me of his fundamental goodness. But his intentions are not honourable.

My great-great-great-grandfather is collecting heather from the roadside to make broomsticks.

He looks up as I approach, takes in my stuck-in-molasses run, my newfangled hiking boots, my pumping arms, furrowed brow, and beaded sweat.

Where are ye aff tae, hen? he asks.

Bad man, I manage, between wheezy breaths. Back there. I flap my arms behind me, refuse to turn my head.

Och, says my great-great-great-grandfather. There are enough of those in the world.

He beckons me down into the ditch. We crouch together in the bracken. His cheeks are pink like mine, rouged with work and effort.

Ye're better aff hiding than running, he says. Then he lifts himself up over the edge of the roadside, peers into the distance. I don't see him, he says. Let's move. He tucks the heather he has collected into his rucksack and takes my hand. We'll go across the moor to the black house, shall we?

I nod.

But after a couple of steps we begin to sink slowly, suckingly, into the bog. The peaty mud is cool on my skin and I am not afraid. As we sink, my great-great-great-grandfather holds my gaze. I see my future and my past in his unruly eyebrow hairs as we travel down through the layers of the earth, closer and closer to the centre of it all.

It's hot in the centre of the earth, but we do not feel the molten lava-ness as heat.

Are we in the middle of the earth's love? I ask my great-great-great-grandfather.

Yes, he says. When people chase me from their doorsteps, when coppers beat me, when your great-great-great-grandmother looks at me with a large sorrow choking her, I come here, to the centre.

Oh, I say. This is a good secret. The earth's love.

I do not tell my great-great-great-grandfather that a large sorrow will go on choking his family for generations. He is a door-to-door salesman, a fixer of cast-offs, a man who knows how to hide from bad men, a make-doer who operates just this side of the law. It is likely he understands the hand-me-down nature of a choking sorrow.

Shall we go back the noo, hen? he asks me gently.

What happens if we don't? I ask.

The earth's love will burn ye up, he replies. He plucks at his braces and adjusts his tweed cap.

Come, he says. I have broomsticks to fashion.

## Wants and Needs

I meet my dead dad at the corner store
where my husband buys cigarettes
for himself and popsicles for our kids.
My dad is wearing a clever costume; he looks
exactly like the owner of the store, a Korean woman
whose mother-in-law has been moved from the ICU
to alternative-level care. But, she says, we cannot afford
this and my mother-in-law has—how you say—mental
disease and she tears out the tubes, she says they are worms,
and her blood pressure is not stable… My dad's eyes
are shiny as chip packages and she is ignoring the line-
up behind me and I know we all have our needs—
I need streetcar tokens and that guy needs
a lottery ticket and I try to teach my children
the difference between wants and needs but who
the fuck knows sometimes? Later, out on the street,
which is dank with November and snoozy leaves,
I will walk with tiny purpose, thinking about
poems and the mucus that seeped from my daughter's
ear in the night and I will meet my father again
in the form of a stout, ruddy-faced man in construction
boots who smiles at me as if we have already met
but he knows we have never met and is delighted
by the puzzle of this.

## This party is going to be super!

But only if Joe remains supine
And Suzie stops her pining
And Allan drinks more wine
And Milena sticks to her own kind
And we use furniture for kindling
And pry out each other's fillings
And make a new cage for the foundling
And beat our better natures down
And settle deep into the dawdle .
And sort the even from the odd
And eat potato chips instead of art

## Einstein wrote a letter to his daughter

Such was the law of the entombed teenager.
Oh, sadness that blossoms into many-petalled rage.
Don't sit too long on those green-lipped laurels.
Go out to the movies! The screens are so looming
and the popcorn boxes contain multitudes.

Also, the world is ending in twelve years.
This is not hyperbole; it is peer-reviewed proclamation.

Einstein wrote a letter to his daughter in which he
referenced love as the world's greatest untapped resource.
Sounds so corny. Calvino said it better:
*Find what is not inferno and give it space.*

Roll the stone from the tomb, zitty lover of second-rate hip-hop;
come out into the light, be resurrected! We need you now
with your overlooked empathy and uneven indignation.

When the oceans rise and the skies go tubular,
we will call on you for love and invention.
We will wash your feet
with our ye olde tears.

## Isle of Lewis Poem

*I*

the ferries ferry people
into the island's patient
mouth and if you want
to know where they've gone
you can ask the fairies

that fellow mired in tweed
will tell you stories of shiny
rocks, shifting plates, patient
weather, obsessive seals, seas
that spit and churn

he will sell you a trinket
for some silver and a slice
of your slick
disbelieving
soul

*II*

There is a man
in a nearby town
who would creep
into his neighbours'
houses while they
were working, drink
their liquor, lounge
in their chairs.

The neighbours
returned home
shook their heads
and did nothing.

In a different town
in a different language
we would call this
*enabling*.
Here they call it
*Och, well.*

*III*

I saw Donald Trump's cousin on the bus. This sounds like the beginning of a joke (or a dream) but it is not. Donald Trump's cousin and I rode the bus with my mother-in-law Chrissie Bel. The bus was mostly full of older people at 10 in the morning, and as we approached Chrissie's stop, near her work, she leaned over and whispered to me, "The bloke in the bonnet across from you—that's Donald Trump's first cousin. Donald Trump's mother is from Lewis." I would have called that bonnet a toque: grey, bobbly, and worn, a white nordic pattern around the edge. The man wore black pants, a dark coat that might have been leather. He spoke occasionally to the man seated beside him, another old fellow with a round, red nose. I looked at his profile and really saw the resemblance. Maybe because my exposure to orange-skinned Donald has been through TV news and reality shows, he actually seemed to be a different species to this man I saw on the bus. And yet! There was the same profile, the glower waiting to happen. The man on the bus looked like any number of old *brodachs* you'd see having a bacon roll at the café or peering out the front window to see who was coming up the road. I thought of Donald ranting about women and Mexicans, Muslims and poor people, tweeting non-sequiturs, fomenting rage and small-mindedness, squeezing the earth in his palm like a stress ball. Then I looked out the window. There are no bright colours here, even when it's sunny— the moor and beaches are muted and the blues, yellows, browns, and greens fold into each other in perpetuity. The sky is always moving overhead; the light dapples and dims, then bursts through the clouds in great columns of clarity.

## I invite Joni Mitchell into my dream

I invite Joni Mitchell into the dream where I am making out with
my high school boyfriend on a ratty sofa in a little back room
of his basement. I am afraid of his mother, who is beautiful,
Ukrainian, and witch-like, and worries that he will knock me up
and throw away his life on some Scottish heathen.

Hello, Joni, I say, and she just laughs and lights a cigarette,
perched on the edge of the sofa. Oh, great, I think, now the high
school boyfriend's mother will also blame the smell of smoke on
me, but I don't say anything to Joni because she is like the Queen,
only way more imaginative.

The high school boyfriend's hands are moving up under my
shirt and I am getting a really good feeling in the underwear
zone but I am also getting kind of uncomfortable because Joni
Mitchell is watching. I block the high school boyfriend's hand
and use my dream power to freeze the situation so I can chat
with Joni Mitchell.

Welcome to my dream, Joni, I say.

Huh, she says, and laughs again, all gravelly and real. Why'd you
invite me into this one, honey?

I shrug and look over at high school boyfriend, who is still frozen,
eyes closed and hands twisted and wizardy from being up under
my shirt.

I don't know, I say. Maybe because you wrote the lines *You turn me on I'm a radio I'm a country station I'm a little bit corny* and I sometimes thought you said horny and maybe that was your point—that corny and horny are not that far apart?

Joni laughs for the third time. Y'know, I'm not a feminist, and women mostly piss me off, right?

Yes, I say. It's okay.

Joni pokes the high school boyfriend in the upper arm. He's cute, she says.

Yes, I say. Every time my dad sees his size 13 shoes lined up in our hallway, he says, That fella sure has a good grip on Canada.

Joni laughs for the fourth time. I think I might like your dad, she says.

He's dead, I say, but he has this little pied-à-terre in my heart. He plays basketball in the afterlife, I add.

Yeah, Joni says, I was black in another life. There is an awkward silence because we are both lying and being completely honest.

Joni finishes her cigarette and lights another. The smoke settles in my clothes, clawing at my eyes. I know I don't have much time left.

Did you write the album *Hejira* for me—knowing that when I was 29 I would move to Bowen Island and spend most of my time sitting on a gigantic boulder playing it over and over on my yellow CD Walkman? I ask.

Yes, she says.

I thought so, I say.

I poke my high school boyfriend in the upper arm and he falls over like a toppled statue.

## Accident

Night unspools. Dun-coloured deer frozen
by the rush of us, our rental car. Then gone.
Not ghostly, but skittish with spirit.

Up ahead is the true crash. A car carried a couple. Others
have corralled, cut her out of the driver's seat, devoted
craftsmen bent to the task. I fell asleep, says the man, a small
black bag clutched to his chest. I woke up upside down.

In his hand, a plastic comb. The tininess of travel scattered
in the ditch: paper pouch of shampoo, glint of razor,
red bandana, rolled and knotted, shards of wind-
shield, toothpaste tube. In the blink of hazards, the man stoops
and straightens, harvests strewn stuff from the roadside.

The woman's face is the flat yellow
of a riverbank, her speech slurred.
She points to where the steering
column pressed into her breast. Holds fast
to a stranger's hand.

You turn the key, light the dash, turn signal *tchik-*
*tchiking* us back into traffic. The silence is slender;
silver aspen in the front seat.

# Quartette

*Alison*

Alison said, "I don't want it, except for tired." The longest
conversations asked for another sip of water. "You know, drugs
aren't blurted ahead. I smoked that beat me up." Her father
simply nodded pillow. "What's in those like it?" "You're not mad,
brown plastic bottle?" "I'll get mad later." She heard on the bed
as though some water running up. She looked around. Suddenly
her there without being much.

*Beverley*

Horizon is really important to me
and Patches the Cat who is on his way out.
I share my marijuana oil with him and
use doggy walking as dialogue.

Mary McCormick has a heated pool.
In the spring the ice melts off the lake.
I will always say yes to brandy and breaststroke
and would chew on chunks of tree,
sky, and lake if the cupboards were bare.

*Frannie*

Frannie looked much better. But there was a toughness that the morning was hanging in. And she looked like she'd eaten something clear or something like that. Can you imagine that? The street lights in the lower avenues were humans like the rest of us. At least a little bit flaky, for sure too unstable to move up in the hierarchy. Particularly tired, stood up. Almost suckered by sincerity.

*Renata*

The flag was more a pennant really—green, triangular, smallish. It had been plastered to a rock by the surf but broke free when a wave sent a dessert plate crashing onto the beach. The dessert plate was remarkably intact save for a semicircular bite-sized chunk missing from the edge. Faded orange markings radiated from the centre of the plate like a child's sun. The fire extinguisher had landed upright and was planted firmly in the moist sand. Renata, watching a seagull, loved egg salad sandwiches. Always had, ever since Auntie Sandy made them with more mayonnaise than she was used to one lunchtime in Grade 4, back when they lived on Traymore Crescent.

## Nobody Told Me

Nobody told me that after I had children I would one day discover a new app on my phone called The Moron Test.

I have learned to watch certain men like televisions.

Nobody told me to pick up lactose-free milk.

I have learned that cats are good dancers.

Nobody told me that people just go right on dying.

I have learned that the trick is to turn the thing around.

Nobody told me time moves like a drunken belly dancer.

I have learned that I am the large pink part.

Nobody told me my future husband would hate having his feet touched.

I have learned that outside the tent is only wind and wild things.

Nobody told me about the surprise birthday party.

I have learned to count cows from the car.

Nobody told me how much fun The Moron Test app is. I had to find out when I was bored on the streetcar on the way to my chiropractor appointment.

I have learned that low-slung belts make you swagger.

Nobody told me that some nightmares consist only of poorly packed suitcases.

I have learned to keep chocolates in my pockets.

Nobody told me I would one day visit a chiropractor.

I have learned that flags are security blankets or king's robes.

Nobody told me email was a gateway drug.

I have learned that the shorter gangsters take fewer precautions.

Nobody told me not to eat the pomegranate, the apple, the cold, sweet plums.

I have learned to swim but not to drive.

# Self-Portrait, a series

*after Joe Brainard*

## I Sink

Loose lips sink ships and I sink so too.

## My Kneecap

Something tore in behind there and sometimes it hurts like a ghost is sticking knitting needles through the adjacent flesh.

## Download Bonus

I click on a lot of things.

## Temporomandibular Joint

I went to a specialist and her assistant gave me a stack of popsicle sticks bound with elastic bands to help stretch my locked jaw. My insurance didn't cover the full cost of the visit and some of my granola still gets knocked off my spoon when I eat.

## Truth Sidewalk

Walk it, baby, walk it.

## Heart

There is good and bad cholesterol; confusing.

## Feeling Ceiling

When I reach it I like to read police procedurals full of laddish detectives from the U.K. who spend a lot of time in rundown pubs having lager-fuelled epiphanies.

## Don't Ask Me How This Happened

Dinosaurs were mean but practical.
Even if I'm here today
it doesn't mean part of me's not extinct.
Roosters make different sounds in different languages.
Right, left, right, left, left my wife and forty-nine kids
somewhere out in Etobicoke
where the squirrels yodel for their mamas
and fascists have finally gained a foothold.

# Dreaming Fidel

*I*

Castro as a young man looks like a clean-cut boxer with his knobby out-of-joint nose, then an imperfect chubby Errol Flynn when he grows the thin moustache, and later still, in profile, somewhat regal, more seasoned. As the beard comes in, the moustache grows to meet it; the fatigues fit like a second skin. And there are the hats: the peaked pillbox army cap he wears on the sports field and while leaning close to hear the greetings of important heads of state, the revolutionary beret pushed to the back of his head like a relaxed tea cosy, the wide-brimmed straw sun hat he dons for cutting sugar cane with the campesinos. His eyes are not wide. When he is not smiling, they are guarded and sad. When he begins to smile, they soften like ripening fruit. Sometimes he uses them to peer up through the cigar smoke that rises from his lips like steam from a kettle set to boil. As an elder statesman, out of the spotlight, he wears track suits, regardless of occasion. Is this a concession to capitalism—the distinctive brand markings snaking down both his arms? Or an acknowledgement of the importance of comfort, a rebellion against formality, the authority of the uniform? He still has good teeth, strong and even—not as square as his friend Che's, but still, they crowd his mouth like the faithful, pressing forward when he smiles or sneers. They understand the importance of clenching, how it can set the jaw with purpose, propel a person forward into action.

Fidel and Che are on a fishing boat. The sun is strong on their young men's shoulders, it beats down on their uncovered heads, but there is a breeze too, and the waves rock the boat as if it were a cradle. Fidel stands at relaxed attention, almost at ease. The men have been talking for a long time, about their plans, their boyhoods, the women they would most like to bed and the women they would trust to mother their children. They are through with talking, although the impulse is still there; every now and then one will signal the other, with a throat clearing or a single word— *entonces*—then fall silent. The boat rocks, the sea rocks them. Fidel is still fishing, but Che lies on the deck, a book open on his chest. Fidel feels a tug on his line and jerks the rod toward him, but it is a nibble only. He thinks of Hemingway's masterpiece—that allegory of man's might, his individual power. And he understands it, he does: as much as he might champion the collective, it is the individual leader who must galvanize the whole. Revolution is not cooperation but an operation. Lenin said it: the bourgeois state must be razed to the ground. Fidel imagines it as a gentler enterprise—controlled. He sees himself on a long bench as if seated at a school lunch table. He is sitting next to Batista, who is at the end of the bench. There is food, laughter, communion. It is history's table. It is not hard to do what he must do, although it is decisive. It is not even cruel, only necessary. He shifts his buttocks to the right forcefully, pushes the man from his seat. Batista falls to the ground with a soft thud, and Fidel makes no move to help him. He turns back to the table. There will be more thudding bodies, he knows, but this first is the most important. There is another tug on his line and this time Fidel knows it is real. He reels the fish in with control, keeping a firm grip on the rod. It is a tarpon of a good size. A far cry from Hemingway's marlin and surprisingly meek, yielding. No matter. Battles are seldom fought in this way, one-on-one, the sun a spotlight. His battles will be more complex, he knows, his enemies shadowy, myriad.

Che has roused himself to watch his friend reel in the fish, unhook it, slit it open with a stout knife he has pulled from his fatigues. He loves his friend's integrity and blunt ruthlessness, knows it will be necessary. He too has been daydreaming to the beat of the sea. But his dream is short, if not simple. He lies in a hammock, having saved one person. He is resting in the knowledge that one fewer person is suffering, although he knows this can never be enough.

Fidel appears to me in miniature, a tiny perfect replica of his human self, and yet somehow more human, more condensed for his smallness, for his perfect shrunken form. In height he is no taller than a kneecap, in girth no wider than a bicep. He is dressed in his trademark fatigues, at his peak, not yet grizzled in beard or filmy of eye. Small, yet incredibly, terrifyingly mighty. He strides over to the base of a mature tamarind tree, leans against it casually, surveying the area beneath the tree, the large shady circle that is his immediate domain. Then he lowers himself to the ground, sits relaxed under the noonday sun. In the background, women, white and black, peel cassava, laughing. Fidel's prisoners languish in snug, strange dens. The dens are small, hollowed out, womb-like havens for hibernating creatures, except that the men who inhabit them have no hope for spring, none of the heaviness in their limbs that connotes bone-deep relaxation, rejuvenation, welcome balm of sleep. The prisoners curl into themselves beneath him; their consciences wither as they reach out to touch the earthy sides of their cells. Above, in the sky, Soviet and American fighter jets drag banners marked with undecipherable slogans. Fidel salutes the jets, peers lovingly at the working women, at the schools and hospitals lined up in the distance. Even in repose he has the look of guardedness and glory that comes from bearing a vision of greatness for so many years. He is so small though! How did he become so small? No matter, it is not long before a flock of doves, pure white, their delicate heads swivelled toward their master, their piercing, adoring eyes fixed on his countenance, come swooping in from the Sierra Maestra mountains. Three of them separate from the flock, approach El Jefe as courtiers, heads bowed. When Fidel nods, the birds take their positions, one at each shoulder.

The other lands, deferentially, a few feet behind him. When he nods for the second time, they use their claws to grip his olive uniform. Within seconds the doves are aloft, carrying Fidel like a doll back to his guerrilla hideout. His tiny legs dangle beneath him. His is a ridiculous exit, but he shows no fear or sense of shame. He rises and rises until he is nothing but a speck against the sun, a tiny, mighty Icarus fading from view.

*IV*

*Questions for Fidel:*

1. What were you like as a boy? Does your boy-self ever intrude, like a bossy dream, upon your competent, resourceful, adult-self?

2. How is it you can order the imprisonment of men and women who, like you, must feel a certain searing, a particular burning in their core? It is a burning that feels like righteousness. Where does that burning originate?

3. Where would you most like to vacation?

4. In which ways do you love your wife?

5. Are you a strong swimmer?

6. What are your feelings regarding fossil fuels?

7. What are your feelings regarding desserts?

8. There are insects that look like sticks in this world, and birds that can blend into flowers. Do you ever want to do the same, or does it bother you a little that they do not have the courage to make themselves known?

*Possible Answers/Theories:*

Above all, Fidel is a parent. Father to the revolution. The revolution is Fidel's boy. Fidel protects the revolution as a parent would a child. He nurtures and feeds it; he allows it opportunity but understands also that its survival is more important than any freedom he might grant it. The boy carries a slingshot and a spade. He loves his father but dreams of his death. No, no, the revolution is a girl. Like a girl, she might, when she reaches a certain age, adolescence, say, flirt and giggle, become overly credulous, believe in ciphers, indulge in shrieks and far-fetched stories. A girl is clever; a girl feasts on the most bloated form of attention, becomes both superficial and inward-looking. A young girl plays hopscotch with the others but also plots behind their backs, is adept at sparking friendships then stomping them out. She reads books. Her brain is not fully developed but her sense of injustice is keen. None of this is her fault. She is lonely and lovely and her feet are always dirty.

## I invite teal into my dream

It is the dream where I invite colours into my dream.

I love teal so much; she is a grimier version of turquoise. And turquoise is annoying; he totally thinks he's all that.

Teal is stocky and handsome. She leans against a tall café table and tumbles a glass vase off the edge.

But don't worry! She catches it before it hits the floor.

My bad, she says, and tips her hat at me.

## Notes Toward a Poem on Jack the Ripper

Tim and I, at six, catching crayfish
and tadpoles among the long
reeds and Coke bottles.

Tim and I, at four, playing
the pull-your-pants-down game in the bushes
while our mothers picnicked and loved us.
We had different bodies.
We were best friends.

Alysa and I, at eleven, our fingers entwined,
laughing and shrieking at the man who came
from the ravine, his sheepskin coat open to
reveal a pink periscope of skin.

Springtime, the salmon struggling
upstream, dodging hooks, fighting waves.

The summer Alysa's mum found a dead body
while walking her dog. He had been sniffing glue.
Still had the plastic bag cinched around his neck.

October, and the man on the radio repeats
a police report: Étienne Brûlé Park,
nighttime, and women.

The winter the river transformed magically
into a landscape of right-angled ice.
There were warning signs that year.

## Bawling Is a Thing My Five-Year-Old Does

*I had a sad dream but I don't remember it.*
When her Minecraft guy falls behind the bed.
*I had another sad dream, but I can't tell you it because it's too sad.*
When her sister makes her sparkly cards and tries to hug her.
*There was tape on the moon. Someone taped up the moon.*
My brother-in-law Joel's Hallowe'en costume.
*And the people were all outside. They were outside of their houses.*
A really bad headache in her tummy.
*There were ghosts. They were ghosts.*
The common and particular way knee-skin skids on sidewalks.
*The people were ghosts?*
Walking alone on a very high bridge.
*Yes, all the people were ghosts.*
When she is so right inside her head and so wrong outside of it.
*And someone taped up the moon?*
Unfair distribution of M&Ms.
*The people were ghosts and someone taped up the moon.*

# Legs

"She's got legs, and knows how to use them!"
—ZZ Top

It is possible to buy pantyhose
nestled in an egg. When you pull
them out, they look like deflated
amputated limbs. Fetal and premature.
Not so when you slide them
onto your own legs. A slick second
skin, smooth and synthetic to the touch,
they will make your calves irresistible
to kindergarten children
and sometimes men.

There are other uses for pantyhose.
For example, my mother once used hers
when the haggis burst
before a Robbie Burns party.
She scissored the hose in two,
scooped the sausagey bits
into one leg, then knotted the whole
thing up to prevent spillage. The Scots
have always had to be resourceful, she said.

## What I'd Like to Believe and What I Know

are two squadrons facing off like spitting frogs
across a swamp in a marble square on an island near Africa.
Myself—some fortunate whose clothes match, yearning for caffeine
and understanding. In the Casa de Colón a pair of live parrots
draw more Germans with video cameras than the fiats and flotillas.

To be cowed by possibility is a luxury,
I know, but you seem about as common as hen's teeth, out-
rageous and useful. Something or someone culled from a fable
who appears through a crenellated arch, repeating yourself
and smoking too many cigarettes while the wind blows
veined and powdery leaves from the trees.

If I could tweak this situation, give it something lissome,
there would be a star called Costner or Cruise, and a long-haired girl
in shades. Continents would heave and hover and we would scoop
scupperfuls of ocean with our bare hands to bring these rafts
of land close. History would end with a tiny pair of leg irons
clattering to the courtyard floor—a pair of parrots nuzzling mid-air.

## Racism invites himself into my dream

It is the dream where I am the only pinky-white-skinned person in an auditorium full of beigey-brown-skinned people who are actually just people. I am sitting in an aisle seat because I am an anxious person with a twitchy bladder.

God is the featured speaker. God is an ash-grey mourning dove. God is the smell of caramel custard. God can tap dance like a motherfucker. God is actually not that compelling as a speaker but there is something about them that makes us pay attention.

Racism walks right up to me. You are an angel, says Racism.

No, no, no, I say. I am not.

Denial, says Racism. Not just a river in Egypt. Look at your limpid blue eyes. The pearly humps beside your spine where wings were once attached!

Betcha you're a schoolteacher, Racism whispers. Don't wanna draw too straight an arrow to an obvious pop culture reference, but: can you say Michelle Pfeiffer?

And oh, it is so true, I have often yearned for those blades for cheekbones.

I invite Michelle Pfeiffer into my dream.

Told you, says Racism, when she comes striding through the doors at the back of the auditorium.

But Michelle Pfeiffer is like the ghost of Hamlet Senior in Act III of the play. He is there to whet Hamlet's "almost blunted purpose"—but only Hamlet can see him and in the meantime his mother is freaking out because Polonius is bleeding out next to the downed arras, which is actually just a fancy curtain. Is the ghost in Hamlet's head? Nobody knows.

This is Racism's sneaky way.

He will make you notice Michelle Pfeiffer—he will make you invite her into your dream—when there is a whole room full of humans with bloody hearts and things to say lined up on either side of you.

Michelle Pfeiffer, I say, maybe you didn't know what an insidious stereotype you were perpetuating in the film *Dangerous Minds*, when you used your tough white-lady charisma to save poor misguided coloured kids, but I think it might be a good idea for you to leave.

Michelle Pfeiffer smiles a saturnine smile and does a little scuffle dance.

I like your boots, I say. But scram.

The woman sitting beside me—large body, large afro sprinkled with white—leans over toward me. Girl, she says, you holdin' discourse with the air. And some people—she jerks her chin left, forward, right, to indicate the assembled crowd—some people tryin' to listen.

Racism just shrugs his shoulders like the French. *C'est la vie*. Then he sits cross-legged in the aisle and pretends to be attentive.

God is singing out the names and addresses of every living creature in the whole world in a language all their own. I find if I close my eyes and stay very still, there are some words I can understand.

# Hades

*for Pamela Adlon*

This morning I choked on my fish oil capsule, died, and was transported to the afterlife. I found myself on a date with Hades, god of the underworld.

Hades was sexy in the way of guys I am not normally drawn to—sculpted and strong. I liked the fact that he could overpower me and likely would, given the chance. Still, I knew better than to meet him on his turf. I chose a vegan restaurant in Parkdale, which I was pretty sure would throw him off his game.

I got there early and sat facing the door. When he arrived the whole place turned to watch. Hades had an appealing underworldly residue about him, even though the day was bright and clear. He was olive-skinned, green-eyed. His gaze was syrup: distilled charisma of politicians and psychopaths.

The thing about emotional labour, I said, is that it is invisible, possibly unquantifiable in the traditional sense, unlike data-driven educational reforms or, I dunno, money. So that when a woman tries to itemize it in computer spreadsheets, or scrawls it in lists on the back of school permission forms, or tattoos it onto her eyelids, no one really takes her seriously. It's like trying to describe the symptoms of perimenopause.

Tell me, said Hades, leaning forward so our noses almost touched. What's good here? I was thinking the sugar snap pea and carrot soba noodles. But the kale, black bean, and avocado bowl also holds a certain appeal.

I knew what Hades was trying to do, but he was right about the avocado bowl. The server wavered a little when she took our order. For fuck's sake, I thought, just because he's immortal. Hades was really, really good with chopsticks. I wanted to bed him too but I had things to say.

So, one of my favourite thinkers opined in a podcast that all mothers are actually single mothers because of this very thing. And, I mean, would it be so hard to just stand beside a person and notice the list? To sidle up and breathe a little while the list is scrolling? Not even shoulder the burden. Really, just to be there would be a boon.

Here, said Hades, try this. He removed a single sugar snap pea from its casing, pinched it gracefully between his chopsticks, and held it up to my lips. His green eyes held mine. I forgot the rule about accepting food from underworld gods and took that pea into my mouth like a pearl.

Hades smiled. He took a sip of his smoothie.

I began to gag and retch, tears streaming down my face. My body, that trusty steed, did its work, dislodging the fish oil capsule, which flew from my mouth in a perfect 180 degree arc and landed intact on my dirty hardwood floor.

The capsule gleamed golden as I breathed in the earth's air. I kicked it under the stove, even though part of me felt sad that all those oils, so fastidiously extracted, would never again be re-absorbed.

## There Should Be No Obstacle

More raspberries
in the colander, please.

There should be no obstacle
to this sweetness.

Partitioned and hairy—
you can wear them

as hats on the tip
of your tongue.

So much is shit these days.

But we are here, and
so are the raspberries—

# Fate

Fate was too intense to train much at first.
He nipped at two or three people, and the sights
and sounds of the suburbs, especially buses and

sirens, drove him to a high and troubling state of arousal.
He wasn't jealous of all men, he had a hierarchy.
His conversation was banal, I don't know, about

the sea, the sky, the seagulls, but it was evident that
he was playing a role, the one he thought was right for me.
In a sense the same reality applies to elephants in the circus.

I don't mean to suggest that all carriage drivers
are perfect, saintly people. He was lighting a cigarette,
the flame leaped up into his face.

At the end he said, pointing to the bed: "You go there, I'll settle
on the cot." It was a mean statement that wounded me, I tried not
to think about it. Fate came from a high-octane herding line.

He broke through screens, climbed through the gate, and pursued
smaller dogs, frightening people walking with their children. Then
he went on to praise the modernizing force of my novel.

## Library Poem

I meet Bob Mackowycz on the way
to the washroom in the High Park
Library. He is holding a bag of books.
Most of them, he says, are for my
daughter, but this one—he pulls out
a book of poetry—this one is for me.
I tell him about the book I am reading.
Borrowed from this same library,
it is a journalist's account of coal miners,
fruit pickers, and cheerleaders in the guts
of America. It interests me, I say, because
my dad was a coal miner in Scotland
before he came here. I didn't know
that, Bob says. Will you write about this?

I look over at the shelves full
of books that people have requested
and that other people have located
on other shelves and transported
to this location, then set carefully
down in the right place so the correct
people can run their fingers lightly
across the spines, mouthing the numbers
until they find the right combination,
the call number! Wa-*hey*! It is, as
the kids say: *Mind. Blown.* Hands
exploding from the tops of their heads.

Sometimes I just want to make out
with the library. Which
reminds me. I once kissed Bob Mackowycz
when we were much younger and less worn.
It was on the porch of my childhood home,
in one of the shoulder seasons. Was it raining?
Possibly. The sun was only half-assedly bright.
Perhaps it was evening.

I have tried to write about that, I say.
But I am not that, I mean, I am not
a coal miner, even though that is part
of me.

Then we talk about the problem of
the internet, how all the modems have
to break down for a real story to happen.

Otherwise, a front-porch kiss might
take the form of a perfectly round yellow
emoji, its lips puckered into a tiny red
heart of possibility, and never be flung
forward into a moment 30 years later
next to the circulation desk by the
washrooms of the High Park Library.

## Spankings

Spankings used to be a thing and they are not anymore
for a lot of good reasons. Here is what I remember
about spankings: once when my sister was still in diapers
but already walking and wilful she picked up my father's hammer,
which was suspended somewhere low-hanging and accessible,
and transported it using her tilted, drunken gait to the sliding
glass door. She was strong in the way of small, sincere children
and people trapped in disaster zones. What was she imagining?
The knock of that blunt-nosed metal against glass. Glorious.
What would happen?
The satisfaction of playing God: to wonder at the world, carnivorous
with curiosity, and conduct experiments outside of civilization.
Glass shattered into stars the like of which she had never seen,
swaddled in her cot as night fell. My dad spanked her hard
on her padded bottom, his voice edged with his own unfenced
imaginings. Another time, at 14, I insisted on wearing
ripped jeans on a family outing
to the Broadway musical *Cats*—"Magical Mister Mistoffelees!"
It was supposed to be fancy and we didn't have a lot of money
for these kinds of things. I was such a little shit, sunk deep
in my own superstitions and signage. My dad raised his hand and
time suspended like disbelief suspends when people
dressed as cats sing and dance onstage.

# 3 Verses About My Long-Distance Relationship

The jarro in the foyer was once full of olivas, you explained,
in a dream, as if it was your job to join me with gem-like
facts hazed by time. That's loony, I said, they're too roomy.
I was wearing chenille and putting on airs.

*

There are nights when the rooster's cry is cast as the *ay-ay-ay* of
a sax, and you seem planted in faraway folds; a toy larch in a limp
landscape, a pregnant pod in the path of an ox, a teenage
beauty caned in India, the starry em of Andromeda.

*

When it comes to poetry, I'm sure there are pie-sellers equal to—if not
better than—a slob like me, caught in the do-re-mi, the fa-so-la, the ti,
a drink with jam and id. What I mean is, roosters are nice, but I miss
Muskoka's loons and wish you'd stop playing tour guide in my dreams.

## Bob Dylan slouches into my dream

It is the dream where I am attending a fundraiser for my older
daughter's dance school in a small local park. Bob Dylan is
crouching next to the slide doing something fiddly with his
hands—smoking maybe?

Oh my god, I say to my husband, Charles. That's Bob Dylan. Do
you think Lori managed to snag him for the fundraiser? What a
coup! I don't know why I am talking like this in my dream. It's
embarrassing. I think you should request a song, I hiss-whisper to
Charles. No, he says. He doesn't look open to requests. Still, I say.
It's Bob. Dylan.

Okay, he says. He walks over to where Bob Dylan is crouching.
Hello, Mr. Dylan, he says. Would you please play "Blowin' in the
Wind"? I am immediately furious. Why so obvious a song choice?
But Charles just shrugs in a way that I know means: You forced me
into this and that song is a classic for a reason and you could have
just left us both alone.

Bob Dylan listens to Charles with frayed patience. Then he stands
up—he is still stooped, shoulders pulled forward in fortification against
the world—pulls a harmonica from his pocket, and begins to play.

The kids dangling off the monkey bars behind him stop for a
moment, then drop like chestnuts to the ground. They slap their
raw hands together, but it is unclear if they are listening. The kid
on the swing does not stop swinging, but instead pushes herself
higher, scooping at the sky with her stubby legs.

My younger daughter rides her skateboard past Bob Dylan. This is so like her. I know that later she will ask me questions to which she knows I have no answers, then insist on the essential wrongness of my response.

Later still she will address me as "milady" to mollify me. She will demand a bedtime snack.

Bob Dylan's thwarted howl of a voice soars up and over the swing set, slide, and scraggly trees. When he is finished, the assembled adults applaud. Whooo! I call out. Bob Dylan!

Bob Dylan ambles off without speaking.

Charles, I say. Why didn't you talk to him, get a selfie or at least an autograph? Charles shrugs again in a way I would find sexy in any other situation. So blasé in the face of celebrity! I'm going to follow him, I say.

Fine, says Charles, and turns back to the potluck table, which is festooned with three-bean chili, gluten-free brownies, and a casserole whose rutted surface has remained stiff and unbroken for the duration of the event.

I catch up to Bob Dylan and follow him all the way to Bloor Street, where I spot him leaning casually against a wall, one leg flamingoed up against the brick. Hello, Mr. Dylan, I say.

Hmmh, he says.

I notice he is staring over to the far side of the road, across the lanes of traffic. The late afternoon sunlight is falling onto the top of the rundown brownstone opposite us like a mist of all that is good and golden.

I take a breath and try for a moment to see what Bob Dylan sees.

There are pigeons on the building's roof. And pigeon shit. And, if I strain and squint, two triangles of pizza, balanced gracefully on their pointed tips, glistening with oil, redolent with perfect rounds of pepperoni.

I glance over at Bob Dylan. Has he seen what I see? He does not look at me. I turn back to the pizza. Wow, I say.

Yes, Bob Dylan says. His eyes do not leave the magnificent tract of light. That's what I call Karaoke Hockey.

## Did You Hear the One

Did you hear the one about the champagne and the scotch tape?
He asked her to hold the mustard.

Did you hear the one about the lemons going in for surgery?
Oh, the sadness of money.

Knock, knock!
Who's there?
Ouch.
Ouch who?
Ouch, yum, phantom peach.

Did you hear the one about how we fear our own purpose?
No.

Have you heard the one about blocked dreams and salty exit signs?
Yes, last night outside the library doors. Margaret told it to me,
and her son, who is autistic and memorizes episodes of CPAC for
kicks and survival, did not find it at all funny.

# Rickshaw

*for Julie*

When I die I will leave you a message
in the woodpile amongst the fungi and
burrowing creatures—sister of mine
who has plastered my soul together
countless times; we were born of bumptious
banter, tinned pea soup, kitchen table
haircuts, Labour Day parades, labours that
stretched through nights and over centuries,
mouldy lasagnas, neck lumps, locked wards
and unlocked laughter, snifters full of hope,
messed-up milestones, fart jokes, sincere and
specious prayers, the nuzzling textures of night.

(We were often overcrowded but
we ravelled each other up.)

It is time to fashion new thinking
caps so we can count the mattress
ads on the subway together.
My kid says 8 + 8 = ROCKS
NEXT TO A RIVER—and I know
that you believe her.

I want to go on billowing
and barking with you forever!
If I had a rickshaw I would carry
you in it every time you moped!

Shoo, splintering sadness and soft
pillow of pain.

## The Others Admitted Afterwards

that they saw the dozy
dignified dog shimmy
along the sidewalk
that there was still
some sense of honour
in the cubbyholes
they called hearts
that the musics that swelled
from their numbskulls
were catalogues of
resignation and woe
that they had each started
a blog to contain—
like vases—the particular
pluck and stringiness
of their thoughts
that it bothered them
a little that the word
*cookie* and the word
*biscuit* signify
the same foodstuff
that it had enthralled them
in French class when
Mrs. Pennell's black bra
strap slid down her shoulder
visible like the cosmos
through the silky trans-
parence of her blouse

that some moods make
you unhappy in houses
and sad on the streets
that they had not
witnessed the home-
coming or the bombing
or the medal ceremony
or the birth or the bris
or the white wedding
or the bluster of her
becoming or the bread
being sliced and tossed
onto plates or the sky
being shredded and
distributed as currency
or the child licking jam
from the jar or the man
wielding primroses or
the raccoon holding court

## Notes Toward a Novel Inspired by
## Frank Wedekind's *Lulu*

Lulu lives in a housing co-op in a sub-development
outside of Edinburgh. She is fifty-four, obese,
with a heart condition, and a dog named Malcolm
who sings along to Rod Stewart albums. Her husband
smuggles cigarettes across the border from France.
He's only been caught twice. Every night, after she has fallen
asleep, he brushes her hair back from her forehead and strokes
her cheek with the tips of his fingers. Her favourite chair
is brown with beige and blue flecks and soft, rounded arms.
She likes tea and kippers on a Sunday morning. Her friends
have voices stronger than vodka and memories the size of iron girders.
They see each other through the smoke at the Bingo Hall.

*

Lulu lives in Chicago, where escaped canaries have made their nests
a nuisance. She is thirteen, dyslexic and hyperactive, but
there is a drug for the latter. So when she takes her dose she can focus
on the six fallen apples for eight fallen women, on the way ginger ale
pinches at her throat until she swishes it gently into her cheeks,
then back through her molars to make it sweet and flat. She can focus
on El Cubanito in the schoolyard, who will pay her five dollars
for a Ritalin pill and sometimes touches her in an alley
behind a dumpster, whispering, *Your belly, your toes,*
*your belly, your toes, chiquitita.*

*

Lulu lives in Andalucia, on the plain, in an ochre-coloured town
called Turre, down the mountain from Mojacar. On Friday nights
she frequents the local Greek watering hole, where a man
only four feet tall plays flamenco. She is small-boned,
with high buttocks and an immunity to the dust that rises
in dense clouds from the rug when she stamps and claps and shakes
to the music. She is unmarried, unharried by time, but weeps easily
for tiny dead things: bald bird fetuses, crushed snails,
a withered bougainvillea blossom.

\*

I dream of things, seldom people. Streets, not bulimic lines on maps,
but true innards, smell and soot. Dark indoors. Spanish screens.
Absinthe. The *clac-clac* of Goll's housekeeper. Her hand across my face,
*foom-foom* of my own brain's blood when she boxes my ears, German
cities seen from the stars, and French words. *Epuisée*, madame, *epuisée*.
Orgasm, stout ale. *Auntie Mary had a canary, up the leg of her breeks,*
the *clac-clac* of tap shoes full of someone else's feet, the *clac-clac*
of applause of her hand across my face, things, seldom people,
thighs and taut canvas, *Bouleversée,* madame, *bouleversée, un chandelle.*
I dream one person. He wears striped suspenders and I am not afraid.

## Advice II

When you write a poem, try
not to mention love or farts
or other things that happen
in elevators or bus shelters;
these clichés
will overwhelm your reader

Here is a conversation I overheard
outside my window late one night:

—You're a slut.
—Go back to your hole, rat.
—Slut.
—You're a rat.
—You're a doped-up slut.
—You're a drunken rat.
—You slut!
—You homeless, drunk rat!

Anything could be a poem
but that doesn't mean anything
should be a poem.

Also, don't use the word *overwhelm*
*ghazal* is okay, so is *flat*, and *silence*
if combined with some jackpot adjective
or cleverly enjambed or suggested
by clouds of white space and

the 4 a.m. breathing of a child
on her way home from

a dream of robots and puppies

## Passover Poem

I invite Elijah (and the Buddha and Dolly
and Mohammed and Kali and Beyonce and
Jesus and Minerva) into my dream. It is
the dream where I am back at Baptist summer
camp on an island in Georgian Bay. My parents,
Marxist-Atheists, have sent me here because
it is cheap. I am eleven and ripe for faith. The songs
are so joyful and chapel is held at sunset point,
the pulpit a stack of flat stones, the pews pine logs,
the vista all peaked water and powerful sky.

As a younger child I recited the "Now I Lay Me Down
to Sleep" prayer from my *Little House on the Prairie* books,
followed it with a litany of places and people I loved,
blew wishes like kisses out my window. Last night
I attended a Passover dinner and the seder plate
included a lemon with the word *orange* scrawled on it
in magic marker. An orange is added to the modern
seder plate (together with bitterness, tears, hope,
and sacrifice) to represent "the suffering of women and gays
omitted from the narrative."

But there were no oranges on hand; besides,
life is seldom so on-the-nose.

I fill stockings and hide chocolate eggs for my children—
even as they grow and pose questions about the rising
oceans and the poor. At the seder, my brother-in-law

explains the plagues and miracles using post-it notes
stuck up on his mother's sideboard. Sometimes
the reminders fall; sometimes they form long yellow tails.
His daughter, my niece, has the sad eyes of her zadie. A son
of Holocaust survivors, Zadie's motto was *Easy does it.*
My husband still wears the stiff leather shoes
Zadie passed on to him for special occasions.

The churches, mosques, temples, and synagogues are always
first to be bombed; the scientists first to be muzzled.

I teach in a secular school system, girls in hijabs, boys in do-rags
or skullcaps, Siddharthas on t-shirts, crucifixes dangled
delicately from necks and ears, all those young legs holding
their people up—long skirts, skinny jeans, or baggy joggers.
None of us leave our allegiances or cellphones at the door.
Once, one of my philosophy students said, only partway
joking, "Wait, first you tell us we're descended from monkeys
and now you're telling us we're fish who learned how to walk?"
Today I found another lump in my breast. Tomorrow,
I will take my children to get their missing vaccination shots.

In the exam room I will ask my oracle—an M.D. and mother
to an eight-month-old—to lay her soft cool hands on my body.

# You Won't Know Me

*I*

You won't know me. Any resemblance
to the woman I was is purely recreational

Any resemblance to the woman I was is purely
wool from the charity shop

has been translated by the internet as a spider
translates desire into a web, a trap, a home

Any resemblance to the woman I was is
a pile of soggy flashcards left on the curb

is nestled in my need to be understood/transported while
eating chocolate hazelnut spread directly from the jar

Any woman to the resemblance I was is purely
trapped in the soft skin pouch/sin pouch under my chin

*II*

My kids have lice. I have lice. Yesterday was minus 35
with the wind chill. Today it is raining. On the way
to the café, on the crusty sidewalk, a woman with a stroller
barrels toward me, grim and haunted.
She meets my eyes and speaks. *It's all gonna fucking*
*freeze tomorrow.* I scratch my head. We are an odd tribe,
mothers. Slaves to little sultans, soothsayers, stupid with serenity.

Last night my seven-year-old tantrummed magnificently,
her face contracted in one brow of woe. *I don't wanna*
*rinse my hair,* she screamed. Okay, I said, let's go to bed.
I was desperate for respite, soft with surrender. *No! I do wanna*
*rinse my hair!* It is like living with Bartleby the Scrivener.
You have to admire the steadfastness, the stubborn
tenacity. But do you, really? Yes, you do. Otherwise.

*III*

To the woman I was is the mother of intention
and invention and necessity's mama too.

You won't know me. Any resemblance to the woman I was
is purely Hard Rock Café, Chernobyl, April 26, 1986.

Any resemblance to the woman I was
is squatting in my urinary tract,

is purely I don't wanna, do you wanna live with them?

A furnace full of popcorn, fruit roll-ups and
that famous YouTuber.

*IV*

Any resemblance to the woman I was

is purely the time you were glad the technology in the café
was too fussy for your beat-up debit card because it meant
you had to run across the street to the bank machine and
on the way you met a poodle who sat like a soldier waiting
for her human but deigned to sniff your outstretched palm
and accept the stroke and scratch you bequeathed her

you won't know me

## Come Here You Gorgeous Cloud

Let your assistant gentle your rapid
Poof! Too many election signs floating above lawns
You can play with an Xbox or a stone; your choice, bro
When the rapture comes I will be sitting on a mountain of
    Hallowe'en chocolate
Chatting with a centipede sawn exactly in half; here lies
    arithmetic
I have always loved the number eleven, shout it—eleven!—
For its two tiny lines that run parallel into eternity
And conduct their own silent séance sessions for personkind

# Conception

It is true; they do flit
dead selves, bits of torn tissue
floating over the Atlantic
those gallons of kiwi-froth

A girl is leaning
into some premeditated wind
I lean against a lamppost
Later, I will spring whole
from the scar in my father's forearm

But now the snow slides
like luggage down
a slant of glass sky
The Atlantic, with its sharp-toothed
sharks, sinewed starfish, buoys her ship

The girl misses her bicycle
her dog, her books. She wants to be a vet
Later, she will take a train
to Montreal, sell greeting cards
in the basement of the Simpsons
department store while I whisper
prophecies into her jug-handle ears

Then I will spring whole
from the scar
in my father's forearm

bloodied and blind
the taste of iron on my tongue

It's Friday and windy
ice piled on guard rails
the taste of iron on my tongue

I will spring whole
from the scar
in my father's forearm

and she will wipe the coal dust
from my eyes
with her closed, clenched fists

## Notes

The dream invitation poems in the book were inspired in part by Grace Paley's poem "I Invite."

"Fate" was extracted entirely from Jon Katz's *Talking to Animals* and Elana Ferrante's *The Story of a New Name*.

In "You Won't Know Me," the opening lines "You won't know me, Any resemblance/to the woman I was is purely" are from "Cardio Room, Young Women's Christian Association" by Karen Solie; the words "contracted in one brow of woe" are spoken by Claudius in Act I, scene ii, of Shakespeare's *Hamlet*.

"Will" is an imagined translation of a poem by Georgian poet Rati Amaglobeli.

The first line of "Einstein Wrote a Letter to His Daughter" (and it's such a good one!) is stolen from a poem I can no longer remember or locate. A prize to the person who can!

The "Dreaming Fidel" series was originally published as a chapbook by Proper Tales Press.

"Bawling Is a Thing I Do" was published in the online journal *Minola Review*.

"Flashman" was published in the on-line journal *The Week Shall Inherit The Verse*.

"Accident" was published in slightly different form in *subTerrain* magazine.

"What I'd Like to Believe and What I Know" was published in slightly different form in *Arc Magazine*.

"Decanted" is after "The Tuller Losses" by Barbara Guest.

"Snow Day Poem" was published in *Arc Magazine*, where it was shortlisted for the poem of the year and won the reader's choice award.

## Acknowledgements

So much of writing is about permission-giving; allowing for mistakes, missteps, for the miscellany of thought and feeling that make us human. Two very special people helped me to find that permission for this book. Watching Andrea Thompson, spoken word maven, work wonders with some of my most reluctant high school students has been a truly transformative experience. She coaxed words out of kids I thought would never find their true voices, and her coaxing brought my own poet-self to the fore. Stuart Ross, a different bird entirely, and a poet who somehow infuses the surreal with incredible poignancy, has shown me the value in hijacking my persistent sense-making machine and staying true to my oddball-self. I thank them both from the bottom of my heart.

Over the years, I have been supported by the Toronto Arts Council, the Ontario Arts Council, and the Canada Council for the Arts. I owe my formation and endurance as a writer, in part, to their support of me and my work. More recently, the folks at Anvil Press, particularly Brian Kaufman, took a chance and gave my poetry a home through Stuart Ross's Feed Dog imprint. Thank you also to Clint Hutzulak of Rayola.com for the wonderful cover.

For listening and reading and understanding, thank you: Barbara Berson, Julie Birrell, Carolyn Burke, Lilian Chau, Kirsti Conway, Nancy Cregan, Patricia DiTillio, Joel Freeman, Margaret Gdyczynski, Alysa Hawkins, Sarah Henstra, Amna Husain, Sue Merrill, Kathryn Walsh Kuitenbrouwer, Naja Pereira, Rami Schandall, Kristin Sjaarda, and Nithya Vijayakumar.

I found space and creative respite at Spark Box Studios (run by Chrissy Poitras and Kyle Topping) and at several branches of the fantastic Toronto Public Library—my gratitude to them!

Thank you to my teacher colleagues, and to my students past and present. Public education is where it's at, man.

Enduring love and thanks to the people I live with (and who live with me): my husband Charles Checketts, my mother Jenny Birrell, and my two daughters, Maisie and Eleanor. They are my persistent anchors and my unlikely hot air balloons. I couldn't float or scurry without them.

And thank you, reader, for giving these poems a place to land.

**Heather Birrell** is the author of two story collections, both published by Coach House Books: *Mad Hope* (a *Globe and Mail* top fiction pick for 2012 and a "CanLit cult classic," according to 49th Shelf) and *I know you are but what am I?* Heather's work has been honoured with the Journey Prize for short fiction and the Edna Staebler Award for creative non-fiction and shortlisted for the KM Hunter Award, the *Arc Magazine* poem of the year award, National and Western Magazine Awards (Canada), and received a notable mention in *Best American Essays 2017*. Heather works as a high school English teacher and a creative writing instructor in Toronto, where she lives with her family. Learn more about Heather and her work at www.heatherbirrell.com.

## Other Feed Dog Books from Anvil Press

"A Feed Dog Book" is an imprint of Anvil Press edited by Stuart Ross and dedicated to contemporary poetry under the influence of surrealism. We are particularly interested in seeing such manuscripts from members of diverse and marginalized communities. Write Stuart at razovsky@gmail.com.

*The Least You Can Do Is Be Magnificent: New & Selected Writings of Steve Venright*, compiled and with an afterword by Alessandro Porco (2017)

*I Heard Something*, by Jaime Forsythe (2018)

*On the Count of None,* by Allison Chisholm (2018)

*The Inflatable Life*, by Mark Laba (2019)

**an imprint of Anvil Press**